ETHICAL LIVING™

ETHICAL
FASHION

JOHANNA KNOX

Rosen
YA
New York

Published in 2020 by The Rosen Publishing Group, Inc.
29 East 21st Street, New York, NY 10010

First Edition

Library of Congress Cataloging-in-Publication Data

Names: Knox, Johanna, 1968– author.
Title: Ethical fashion / Johanna Knox.
Description: New York : Rosen Publishing, 2020. | Series: Ethical living | Includes bibliographical references and index.
Identifiers: LCCN 2017055553| ISBN 9781508180494 (library bound) | ISBN 9781508180500 (pbk.)
Subjects: LCSH: Clothing trade—Moral and ethical aspects—Juvenile literature. | Fashion—Moral and ethical aspects—Juvenile literature. | Clothing and dress—Moral and ethical aspects—Juvenile literature. | Animal welfare—Juvenile literature.
Classification: LCC TT497 .K47 2018 | DDC 178—dc23
LC record available at https://lccn.loc.gov/2017055553

Manufactured in the United States of America

CONTENTS

INTRODUCTION

If you care about the world we live in and want to make it a kinder place, then what you choose to buy is important. Every time you hand over money for a product, you're supporting the businesses that make that product. So it makes sense to buy products from businesses that are kind to animals (including people!) and the world we live in and to withhold support from cruel, damaging fashion. Instead, throw your support behind people, businesses, and practices that care for the world and all its beings.

When it comes to clothes, putting together a cruelty-free wardrobe is a massive challenge—there's a lot to think about. Let's say you're shopping for a new jacket. You've found three you like. One is a leather jacket—but it's secondhand and well worn. You're not giving any money to the business that first made it from a dead animal's skin. You're just making sure a perfectly wearable jacket isn't wasted. Is that still wrong? The second jacket is new and made of cotton—a plant fiber. It's from a small local fashion label that provides employment and decent pay for people in your community. You like that! The only trouble is, the cotton they use is from China. The cotton industry is one of the most polluting in the world; and the fiber was woven in a sweatshop. The third jacket is made from wool sourced from a small family sheep farm that strives to treat its animals as humanely as possible and is certified organic. The jacket is locally designed and made. However, it costs a full week's wages. If you had to choose one of these jackets, which would it be? Or should you keep looking?

There are a range of questions you can ask yourself when you're clothes shopping, such as: Is the fabric made from animals or plants? Or is it synthetic? If it's from animals, how were they treated? If it's from plants, what was the environmental impact of

Which of these jackets are cruelty free? The answer may not be as simple as you would think.

growing and harvesting those plants? If it's synthetic, how does its creation impact our planet? How was the fabric turned into garments—who made them and where? What are working conditions like for those people?

You might also want to think about how the clothes are advertised. Fashion is notorious for promoting unhealthy body ideals—especially for women. Do you want to buy from a company that does that? And let's not forget that the very word itself, "fashion," is associated with the idea that you need to buy new clothes constantly to keep up. Overconsumption is bad for the planet and its creatures. How do we combat this and enjoy what we wear?

Chapter One

ANIMAL FIBERS AND FABRICS

The first human clothes were almost certainly animal skins, but we've come a long way since then.

THREADS OF HISTORY

We can't be sure exactly when humans started regularly wearing clothes. However, in 2003, researchers figured out how to estimate it. They already knew that human body lice had evolved to live only in clothes. That meant that the lice must have evolved around the same time that humans started wearing clothes. If the researchers could figure out when they evolved, that would also reveal when human beings started wearing clothes.

The researchers did DNA tests on body lice and concluded that humans started covering up between forty-two thousand and seventy-two thousand years ago. Some of the first garments were animal skins punctured with sharp tools and laced together with

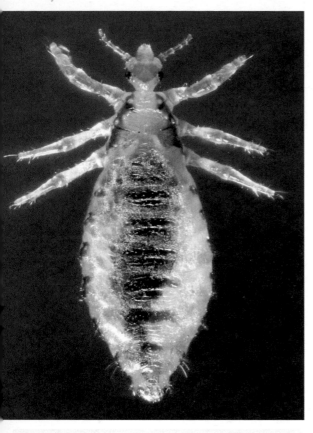

Studying the human body louse (*Pediculus humanus humanus*) has solved the mystery of when humans started wearing clothes. People started wearing clothes many millennia after we lost our body fur.

animal sinews or plant fibers. As humans spread around the world, we started to farm plants and animals for fiber and developed new tools and methods. We spun, wove, snipped, and sewed.

People didn't always have a choice over what they wore. Their clothes depended on the material resources where they lived, their income or bargaining power, and the available garment-making skills. It's much the same these days, although most will have at least some options. The challenge is to use whatever powers of clothing choice you do have to make the world a kinder place.

WHOSE SKIN IS IT?

Leather, fur, and sheepskin are the processed, preserved skins of dead animals. While few people wear real fur these days, there is still plenty of leather and sheepskin around, made into shoes, bags, jackets, and more.

Sometimes an animal has been killed for its skin, but most often it's been killed primarily for its meat. The skin is a by-product. If you don't eat meat but you wear leather, you could say you're fighting only half the problem. For many people who respect animal life, something simply feels repulsive about proudly wearing the remains of a dead animal.

For the environmentally conscious, there is a gray area around animals that are considered pests—like

The brushtail possum (*Trichosurus vulpecula*) has wreaked havoc on New Zealand's native wildlife after being introduced to the country by British settlers who wanted to hunt it for fur.

swamp rats in Louisiana and possums in New Zealand. Both of these animals were taken from their native countries many decades ago and introduced to new lands so that people could use them for fur. However, they were just a bit too well suited to their new environments and overran them, destroying local habitats and wildlife.

In order for local native animals to survive, the swamp rats and possums now need to go, and some people argue that trapping them for their fur is a great way to do that. They say you could call it ethical fur. Unfortunately, a lot of past research shows that trying to get rid of an animal by setting up an economy in which they are hunted for their fur isn't likely to work. Partially, this is because the only way to make the business profitable is by keeping the animal numbers

STICKY QUESTIONS

Most shoes use glue in their manufacture. And a lot of glues are made of processed animal parts. You might see a shoe that looks vegan—that is, it hasn't been made of leather or other obvious animal products. But does it use animal glue?

These days, fewer and fewer manufacturers are using animal glues because there are a lot of synthetic options available. Animal rights organizations like PETA suggest that consumers should contact shoe companies to ask if they can confirm that they don't use animal glues. Not only will you get useful information, but you'll be sending a message to the company that you care about this, and it affects your buying decisions.

high enough to keep hunting them—which, in effect, is not really helping to get rid of them at all.

ANIMAL FIBERS

The animal fibers worn most commonly around the world are silk and wool, but you might come across others in a clothing store, too. Most animal fibers are the fleeces of hairy, wooly, or furry animals. The animals live on farms, where they're shorn of their fleeces once a year or more. The fleeces are then sorted, washed, and turned into yarn or fabric. The exception is silk, which is a thread spun by silkworms. Farming animals to harvest their fiber gives us some thorny ethical questions to think about.

The first domesticated animals were probably sheep. At first, they were farmed for meat, but around 6000 BCE, people in the Middle East began breeding them for their wool, too. Over many centuries, sheep and other fiber animals have been bred to be more docile and to grow ever-better fleeces for human use—softer, stronger, and warmer. These animals have now become dependent on humans, for food and in other ways. Alpacas and domestic sheep, for example, need to be shorn. They don't shed their fleeces naturally anymore, and if they're not shorn, they'll end up dragging mounds of wool around with them, overheating, and possibly dying.

Today, fiber-giving animals are farmed in a wide range of ways. Sheep, in particular, are often raised

on intensive, industrial farms, where they're kept in small pens, fed an unnatural diet, and shorn roughly and cruelly. They live with health problems, and mental as well as physical pain. Goats farmed for fiber and angora rabbits are also often kept in deeply cruel conditions. If you strive for a cruelty-free life, then it's a no-brainer: you'll want to avoid buying clothing made of fiber from farms like these.

But what about more humanely run farms? Around the world, there are many smaller fiber farms—often family run—where the farmers strive to treat their sheep, goats, or alpacas with kindness and consideration. The animals range across wide territories, have social contact with each other, and eat rich diets as close as possible to what is natural for them. The farmers keep an eye on their health, and shear them with care.

Let's take a closer look at what the more humanely run animal-fiber farms look like, and you can make up your own mind about whether they meet kindness standards.

SHEEP FARMS: WOOL

The sheep on a well-run farm live in flocks and graze on lush grass. Rams (males) are kept separate from ewes (females) except during mating season. They're also kept separate from each other, as they fight. There will be many more ewes than rams on a sheep farm, as only a few rams are needed for breeding.

Shearers are well trained, and the ability to shear a sheep cleanly and without hurting the sheep is highly valued. Nonetheless, nicks and cuts do happen. There are always mistakes. For a good shearer, these should be minimal.

While sheep don't die in the process of giving their wool, there is still usually slaughter involved. If a farm is selectively breeding sheep for the best wool and trying to maintain their flock's wool quality over several generations, they will almost certainly be sending at least a few (and sometimes many) sheep—those whose wool quality isn't quite up to scratch or simply those that aren't necessary—to the abattoir. Male sheep get a particularly rough deal here, as farms only want and need a small number of rams.

There's one way to keep a male lamb when there are already enough rams in the flock: he can be castrated. A castrated male sheep, called a wether, can be put with other rams to keep them company without fighting with them, or with ewes, without fear they will mate. Very small boutique farms may have a high number of wethers in their flock, whereas larger farms are more likely to send unwanted sheep to be killed. The castration process is, as you can imagine, painful for the lamb.

Another painful process that all sheep on a farm go through is docking—getting most of their tails amputated. Having a short stump of a tail means a sheep's rump stays clearer of feces, so that they don't get fly-struck. (This is when flies lay eggs in their skin,

A boy on a Utah farm holds a lamb while its tail is docked—a practice that causes distress to the lambs but is considered necessary in modern sheep farming.

which is painful and sometimes fatal.) Docking also makes shearing easier. Studies testing lambs' levels of cortisol—a stress hormone—during docking and castration have, unsurprisingly, shown that the pain is reduced by using anesthetics during and after the procedure. Some farms use such pain relief for the lambs, and others don't.

MERINO AND MULESING

If you've read about animal cruelty, you may well have heard of mulesing. It's not widespread across the wool industry, but when it does take place it's one of the most painful and cruel things to do to any animal— but it's part of a wider story about merino sheep.

Merinos are a breed that produces an extremely fine, soft, warm wool, which is highly sought after for garments. Many of them have been selectively bred to have tough, wrinkly skin. The wrinkles mean that they have a greater surface area of skin—which means more wool. However, this makes them difficult to shear smoothly and painlessly. These sheep also have health problems and are prone to fly-strike. To stop them from getting fly-struck around their rumps, where feces accumulate, some farmers use a process called mulesing: the merino lamb is restrained, and strips of skin are cut away from its hindquarters, often without any anesthesia.

The cruelty of mulesing is widely recognized, and some wool-producing countries, such as New Zealand, have banned it. In others, such as Australia, it is still considered common practice in 2017. When buying merino, look for a product that comes from a country where mulesing is banned or that is certified as coming from a farm where the sheep are not mulesed.

GOAT FARMS: CASHMERE AND MOHAIR

Cashmere is goat fiber from a range of goat breeds, while mohair comes from one specific breed called the Angora goat (not to be confused with the Angora rabbit).

As well as providing fields for the goats to roam, play, and graze in, a humane goat fiber farm will make sure all the animals have shelter and warmth after shearing. Goats have very little body fat, and going into the cold after shearing is miserable for them at best and fatal at worst.

The most humane cashmere fiber may come from combing the goats, rather than shearing them. Combing is considered pleasanter for many goats.

Goats don't get their tails docked like sheep do, but farmers do usually keep a predominantly female flock—with males either being castrated, slaughtered, or sold (possibly to be slaughtered by someone else).

ALPACA FARMS

Good news! There are few—if any—factory farms for alpaca fiber. You can almost guarantee that alpaca fiber is from animals raised on smaller, more humane farms. Alpaca meat is not eaten in most countries, so it's fairly unusual for alpaca farms to slaughter unwanted animals. There is, however, a lot of castration, as, like sheep and goats, fertile males can't generally live alongside one other.

ANGORA RABBIT FARMS

Angora fiber comes from long-haired rabbits called Angora rabbits. Humane rabbit farms keep the animals healthy and stress free. They have clean hutches and room to play. They can be shorn, combed, or "plucked" for their fur, but this is done

Alpacas, closely related to llamas, originated in South America. Today they're farmed in many parts of the world for their richly colored fleeces.

in a careful, kind way—often so that it's like a form of grooming for the rabbit. Angora rabbits produce less fur as they get older. The most humane farms will keep their older rabbits even after they're "retired" and give them a good life until they die naturally.

SILK FARMS

Is there any such thing as humane silk? After silkworms hatch from their eggs, they live on mulberry trees and spend six to eight weeks eating nonstop,

before spinning silk cocoons around themselves, ready to turn into silk moths. However, most silkworms never get the chance to emerge. Unless they're being saved for breeding, the cocooned silkworms are dropped, by the thousands, into vats of boiling water. The dead larvae are removed from their cocoons, and those cocoons are processed into silk.

You might have heard of Ahimsa silk—or peace silk. Some people claim this is cruelty free, as the moths are left to emerge from the cocoon naturally. The quality of the silk is lower because as the moths emerge, they damage the cocoons. But is this even cruelty free? Once these moths emerge, they don't have much of a life. After centuries of selective breeding for larvae that spin excellent silk, the moths themselves are deformed, clumsy, and flightless. The silk farms don't look after them in any way. Generally, the moths are destroyed or left to die, as are the breeding moths once they've fulfilled their task.

Some people might ask, why worry? They're only insects. They can't think and feel the way larger animals can. But when it comes to behaving compassionately toward other living beings, as philosopher Jeremy Bentham has said, shouldn't the only question be, "Can they suffer?" In the case of insects, we don't know exactly what their suffering feels like, but the answer is still, almost certainly.

WHAT CAN WE DO?

Some fiber consumers may feel, all things considered, that they can live with the practices involved in the most humane farms. However, others who are striving to lead cruelty-free lives may not be comfortable with those practices and may even have concerns that are larger than what happens on any individual farm: Should humans be farming animals at all? Do we have any right to exploit nonhuman lives for our own gain?

For some people, nonanimal fiber is the only option. But this isn't straightforward, either.

Chapter Two

VEGAN FIBERS AND FABRICS

A vegan wardrobe isn't necessarily as simple as one that bans clothing from the hides or fleeces of animals. Other than those that come from animals, there are three main types of fiber used in clothing: natural plant fibers, synthetic fibers, and a kind of cross between the two that is often referred to as regenerated fibers. If it's to be truly cruelty free, all the processes used to manufacture a yarn or a fabric need to be kind to the world and its living things as well.

NATURAL PLANT FIBERS

Some plants have strong cellulose "threads" that can be processed and then spun or woven into yarn and textiles. Cotton, linen, hemp, and ramie are the most commonly known.

COTTON

Cotton is the most widely used plant fiber in the world—nearly half of all textile production is cotton!

Even denim is a kind of cotton, woven and dyed in a particular way. But cotton is by no means cruelty free. The World Wildlife Fund says, "Unsustainable cotton farming...has already been responsible for the destruction of large-scale ecosystems such as the Aral Sea in central Asia and the deteriorating health and livelihoods of people living there."

Cotton plants are sensitive to pest and disease, so pesticide use on cotton farms is heavier than on almost any other crop in the world. Although only 2.4 percent of the world's crop land is planted with cotton, it uses 24 percent of the world's pesticides and 11 percent of the world's insecticides. The poisons used on cotton crops spread into the surrounding land and make people and animals sick. Cotton production also wastes massive amounts of water and has left many wetlands and waterways dried up. Although the

A crop-dusting plane flies low over a field of cotton plants to spray them with pesticide. Conventional cotton plantations require enormous amounts of environmentally damaging sprays.

cotton industry has been trying to clean up its act, it hasn't made a lot of progress. Pesticide use has dropped slightly, mostly through developing new genetically modified cotton varieties.

There is a way to buy more sustainable cotton, though. It's more expensive (and has to be), but cotton that is certified organic has a much smaller environmental impact than inorganic cotton. Pesticides are barely used, and although it's still a thirsty crop, it doesn't use as much water. Many people think it's worth throwing support behind organic cotton to encourage more cotton producers to switch to organic methods. (That makes organic denim the kindest choice as well.) And if you also care about ensuring that workers on cotton farms are treated well, you should buy fair trade organic cotton.

HEMP, LINEN, AND RAMIE

Hemp, linen, and ramie, plants that have been used for fabric for thousands of years, give "bast fibers" from their long, strong stems. Ramie comes from a plant in the nettle family; linen from flax plants; and hemp from hemp plants. Each makes a strong, breathable, luxurious, and moisture-absorbent fabric.

Hemp has excellent insulating properties—it's warm in winter and cool in summer. These fibers have a much lower environmental impact than cotton. They need less water to grow and far less pesticide. Hemp even improves the soil that it's growing in, aerating it and removing toxins.

Al Espino owns Hempwise Boutique in Santa Barbara, California. It's one of many hemp clothing businesses that are flourishing as hemp fiber's benefits become better known.

Ramie and linen can be hard to grow in many places, so they haven't taken off in the same way that cotton has and are more expensive. Hemp may prove to be easier to grow—and the hemp industry is currently undergoing a renaissance. While linen, hemp, and ramie are all choices you can feel good about, certified organic is even better!

SYNTHETIC FIBERS

The most common synthetic fibers are nylon, poly-ester, acrylic, vinyl, and spandex. Each begins life as

a pulpy mix of petrochemicals and is then artificially formed into threads, which can then be spun or woven into fabrics.

Petrochemicals are chemical compounds that are extracted from petrol, so synthetic fabrics are dependent on the oil industry. That's the first strike against them. As a major driver of climate change, the oil industry is one of the most dangerous and unsustainable on the planet—affecting every living thing. By buying new clothes made from synthetic yarns and fabrics, you are directly supporting more fossil fuels being taken from the ground.

The manufacturing process for synthetic fibers also uses a lot of energy and water and emits high levels of greenhouse gases. And the problems with synthetic fibers don't end with their sale; the world is realizing that, once bought, synthetic textiles are a massive pollutant, poisoning waterways and oceans and all the animals that live in them.

When you wash synthetic fabrics, they shed tiny hairs called microfibers. These get washed out in your laundry water into pipes and drains and eventually into rivers, lakes, and the ocean. Because they're so small, the usual wastewater filters don't work, and because they don't rot or biodegrade, they accumulate in the environment. They've been found in vast quantities on seashores and other places wastewater is released. Because they're so small, fish and other wildlife easily ingest them. Scientists have found them in fish stomachs. A University of Exeter study

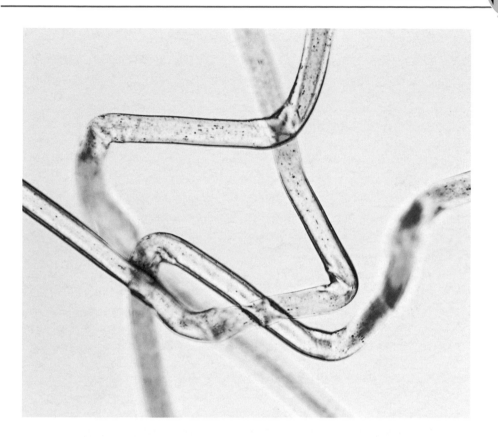

This tiny nylon microfiber—seen through a microscope—looks innocuous. But wash trillions of them into the ocean, and you have an Earth-sized problem.

showed that when crabs eat food containing microfibers, their behavior changes—they eat less, leading to stunted growth.

Perhaps most worrying of all, synthetic microfibers absorb toxins, and whenever an animal eats them, those toxins get into the food chain. A single fleece jacket can release a million fibers during one wash!

ARE THERE ANY ETHICAL SYNTHETIC FIBERS?

About 60 percent of synthetic fiber production is polyester. There are several types of polyester. One is polyethylene terephthalate (PET)—the plastic used for soft-drink bottles. Some enterprising companies have begun recycling PET bottles and turning them into polyester fabric. This is a good thing, right?

Well, it's true that these bottles are being saved from going to the landfill. Producing recycled polyester uses less energy and produces significantly fewer greenhouse-gas emissions than producing new polyester. However, until a solution is found, they will continue to release poisonous microfibers into the environment every time you wash them.

REGENERATED FIBERS

Regenerated cellulose fibers are like a cross between natural and synthetic fibers. They begin as a pulp made of natural plant materials and are then turned into thread using processes similar to those used for synthetics. Unlike synthetics, however, they're biodegradable.

RAYON

Rayon, invented in the nineteenth century and dubbed artificial silk, was the first regenerated fiber. There is still a lot of rayon around today and many different ways to manufacture it—usually from wood chips. Generally, strong toxic chemicals are needed to turn the wood first into pulp and then into delicate thread. The rayon industry produces a lot of chemical waste. If it's not disposed of properly (and often it isn't), rayon poisons the local wildlife and environment. Workers in rayon factories are also at risk from the poisonous fumes that the process releases. Whether the workers and the local environment are treated with care depends on the individual rayon factory, the laws in place in the factory's country, and how well the government enforces those laws.

Some companies have been working on improving rayon manufacturing processes so that toxic chemicals are recycled and reused rather than ending up as waste, and this has been a big step forward. Rayon is also generally made from eucalyptus wood, which is a low-impact tree crop. But all rayon has one additional drawback: it doesn't take dye easily, so large quantities of strong chemicals are needed to color it well. This process is bad for the environment.

If you choose to buy rayon, keep an eye out for Lyocell (the brand name it goes under). It's still currently your most environmentally friendly rayon choice—but, as with many textiles, it's not a perfect choice.

This bamboo forest located in Maui, Hawaii, is hugely beneficial to the planet, removing large amounts of carbon dioxide from the atmosphere. But can it also be made into cruelty-free fiber?

BAMBOO AND SOY FIBER

The most common nontree crops used to make regenerated fiber are bamboo and soy. However, the same toxic chemical issues apply to their manufacture. Bamboo fiber's redeeming feature is that bamboo is often a highly sustainable crop.

Soy fiber is a by-product of the soy food industry, so its manufacture helps reduce waste. However, soy takes a lot of water and pesticide to grow, and many soy crops are GMO.

MYTHS AND FACTS

Myth: Animals have to die to give us their fleece.

Fact: Shearers take the fleece from all kinds of animals (including sheep, goats, alpacas, and Angora rabbits) without killing them, and then they grow new fleece. However, there can be cruelty involved in the process, and some fiber farms do slaughter unwanted animals for meat.

Myth: Plant-based and synthetic textiles are kinder to animals and the planet than animal-based textiles.

Fact: This is true of some plant-based and synthetic materials, but many others devastate the environment and its ecosystems because of the methods used to grow or process them.

Myth: Clothes should be cheap. Expensive clothes are a rip-off.

Fact: Cheap clothes are often cheap because the manufacturers cut corners, ignore environmental concerns and health and safety regulations, and pay their workers way below minimum wage. Clothes that have been created according to strong ethical principles will cost more to buy new. There's no way around it. However, there are other ways to put together a great wardrobe on a budget!

Chapter Three

FROM FABRIC TO FASHIONABLE FIND

It's great to choose clothing made from an ethical fabric, but a lot happens just along that journey from textile to garment on a clothing rack. There are two key industries involved in transforming fabric into fashion: the dyeing industry and the garment production industry. Both are largely based in developing countries where staff (mostly young women) are routinely forced to work extreme hours for pitiful pay in inhumane, often dangerous conditions. These people are trapped in a cycle of extreme poverty, and many consider this a modern form of slavery. The dyeing industry is also notorious for the damage it does to the environment and the world's wildlife.

THE TROUBLE WITH DYEING

The destruction caused by the dyeing industry is completely at odds with the beautiful, cheerful colors that dyes produce. Like synthetic fabrics, most commercial dyes are made from petrochemicals, so are dependent

Wool is brightly dyed in this restored nineteenth-century Scottish textile mill. Synthetic dyes were developed in the mid-nineteenth century and have become an environmental disaster.

on fossil fuel production, which urgently needs to be curtailed in order to slow down climate change.

Commercial dyes are also damaging life on Earth. Cambridge University's *Well Dressed Report* says, "During the dyeing process an average t-shirt will use 16-20 litres of water." In their thirst for water, dye factories often exhaust local water supplies that people, animals, and plants need for survival. The report goes on to claim that "80% of the dye is retained by the fabric and the rest is flushed out… The global textile industry discharges 40,000–50,000 tons of dye into the water system."

Most commercial dyes, and the chemicals used to fix them in the fibers, are toxic and carcinogenic. They destroy life in the waterways that they're dumped into, which then flow into the oceans and spread around the globe. Also, when you wash new clothes for the first time, dye residues often come out in the water and flow through your wastewater systems into your local environment. Keep in mind, also, that dyes give off poisonous fumes—and in many dye factories, workers are not protected.

This all sounds very bleak, but there is one ray of hope for the commercial dye industry: waterless dyeing technologies. Over the past decade, at least three companies have come up with different industrial dyeing methods that use far less water and dump far less toxic waste than older methods. Unfortunately, the problem remains that the technology can cost millions of dollars for a factory to install. This is a huge barrier. The factories already operate at low margins, and few can or are willing to switch to these new, more planet-friendly ways.

That said, a few large companies have begun to make the switch, and an internet search will show you which ones. What needs to happen now is that more companies need to be encouraged to switch, and the costs for the new technology need to come down.

CLOTHING PRODUCTION

In 2013, the Rana Plaza in Bangladesh collapsed, making headlines around the world. This five-story building contained several clothing factories. The death toll was 1,134 people, and more than 2,500 people were injured—many in life-altering ways.

Union lawyer Jyrki Raina says, "Brands were fully aware of the conditions at factories like Rana Plaza but continued business as usual, increasing orders and demanding lower prices." The disaster threw the terrible treatment of workers in clothing factories into stark relief and began a global conversation about the human cruelty involved in the manufacturing of our garments.

As rescuers search for victims in the wreckage of the Rana Plaza, garment workers gather in protest of the conditions that led to the tragedy.

Nonetheless, disasters in clothing factories continue to take place week after week—usually fires or collapses—and they're rarely reported. And working conditions and pay for garment workers in these factories are still routinely abysmal. While awareness has grown since 2013, little has truly changed.

MARKETING: PLAYING WITH OUR EMOTIONS

Once clothes are made, they are advertised and marketed, as conventional businesses want to sell as much as they possibly can and grow. It sounds straightforward, but this simple wish can be deeply

ARE ANY CLOTHES MANUFACTURED WITHOUT HUMAN CRUELTY?

Fair trade organizations (FTO) are working on new business models in which garment workers are paid fair wages, their employment rights are upheld, and the business contributes to the community's well-being.

Many of these organizations are also reviving artisan skills and the use of traditional, nonpetrochemical dyes. They generally have a strong emphasis on environmental sustainability and see the way they treat people and the environment as part of one whole. The range of fair trade fashion available is growing all the time.

Some high-end clothing designers also prioritize how and where their garments are manufactured. Reading articles, searching the internet, and asking professionals in your community can help you find out which companies are working toward these goals.

problematic. Think about what makes you want to buy clothes. What marketing influences you? Ads you see online and in magazines? Reports from fashion shows? Photos of celebrities wearing certain labels? Displays inside shops? How much attention do you pay to each of these? Are you aware of all the messages they are sending you?

You've probably noticed that the vast majority of fashion marketing features models, celebrities, or mannequins who conform to a particular body type. Marketing culture presents these body types as aspirational—even though most people would never be able to look this way. Research shows that after viewing advertisements that promote these appearance standards, many people feel dissatisfied with themselves. Flick through a glossy magazine or wander through a city's fashion precinct and you'll find yourself immersed in this kind of imagery. Is it ethical for any company to promote imagery that feeds on unhappiness and low self-esteem?

Some companies are beginning to make an effort to use models with diverse looks, and these efforts are usually applauded. But do they really solve the problem with advertising? Find some examples and see what you think. Do the models in these ads really represent human diversity, or do they still conform to the beauty ideals that are mandated by society?

Consider advertising in a more generalized manner. A 2011 article in the *Journal of Consumer Research* looked at fashion and beauty advertisements that didn't include images of any human beings but rather were focused on products. After viewing the advertisements, customers still felt less attractive. The study suggested that "advertisements displaying beauty-enhancing (rather than problem-solving) products are likely to remind consumers of their own shortcomings."

The purpose of advertising is, of course, to make viewers want to buy something, and it seems that many advertisements do this primarily by undermining the viewer's confidence and security, which makes them more receptive to being sold something that will, the consumer hopes, soothe those bad feelings.

Whether you're browsing the internet or walking down the street, it's hard to avoid being bombarded by advertising. New York City's Times Square is an extreme example.

All of these issues raise questions about the ethics of advertising fashion and beauty products altogether. When you look at a clothing advertisement, what are you really being sold? An item that you genuinely need in order to stay warm and clothed or an unnecessary addition to your wardrobe that will make you feel good only for a short time before you want to buy something else?

Even the definition of fashion as "the latest style" can be seen as problematic. Do we really need the latest style? Who benefits from the constant pressure to keep up with new fashions? Certainly, the companies who sell fashion items benefit. But we, the consumers, don't. We simply end up trapped in an endless cycle of insecurity, throwing more and more money at the ever-shifting goal of keeping up. This is the very definition of overconsumption. It's a drain on the world's finite resources and creates vast amounts of waste and pollution. That's bad not only for us, but for the planet and all its living things.

Chapter Four

THE POWER OF PURCHASE

When people talk about "purchasing power," they are usually referring to how much money you have to spend. But let's widen the definition. Your consumer power is about more than just what your money can buy.

As a buyer, you can make the world a kinder place. Your choices can influence others around you to make similar choices, and on your own or together with others, you can influence the businesses you buy from to become more ethical because businesses depend on whether buyers want their products.

Your purchasing power doesn't just rest on how much money you have, either. It resides in your knowledge and values and your ability to make informed choices. There are all sorts of ways to influence the fashion world for the better, and it's up to you to choose which ways are best for you.

LESS IS MORE

The most straightforward way to make a positive impact on the world and all its living things is simply to buy less.

This might mean thinking about whether you really need all the clothes you buy. If you don't, then reduce the quantity. The bonus for you is that you'll save money.

Another option is to spend the same amount of money you would normally spend on clothes, but buy fewer, more expensive clothes that will last longer.

Here's an interesting exercise: next time you're shopping for new clothes and see two different garments you want to buy, think about what single ethical thing you could buy instead, for the price of those two. Imagine it as the opposite of a two-for-one deal. When it comes to the planet's well-being, the best deal may be one for two!

SWAP, DON'T SHOP

Some of us just can't help it—we love variety in our wardrobes and get joy from the new. But there are ways to achieve this without constantly consuming products.

This model's trousers are by Kowtow, a New Zealand–based label with an ethical focus. Kowtow's garments are long-lasting, use 100 percent organic cotton, and are produced in fair facilities.

Clothing swaps are becoming increasingly popular. To run one, dig out all of your old clothes that you don't want anymore and invite a group of friends to do the same. Get together and have fun rummaging through each other's stashes. One person's trash is often another's treasure!

If you're feeling more ambitious, you could organize a larger-scale swap in your community, through any group that you belong to or by hiring a venue and putting up notices. If you're concerned about making the swap fair, then use a token system: people get one token for every item they bring and then get to "spend" their tokens on items they want to take home with them.

SHOPPING YOUR WARDROBE

If you have a lot of clothes already, chances are that you've forgotten about some of them. Have a look through everything you own and see if you can rediscover one or two garments that you've neglected—then start loving them again.

Mix and match them with your other clothes in new ways, or wear an item completely differently. Stretchy skirts can be pulled up to make tops. Tops can be worn around your waist as skirts. Pants can have the legs cut off to become shorts.

You could also think about more complex ways to upcycle older items in your wardrobe. The internet is chockablock with ideas for upcycling your clothes and wearing them in new ways. Take a look!

SECOND TIME AROUND

Buying secondhand or vintage is an almost fail-safe way to buy ethically. You can purchase a new-to-you garment while feeling secure in the knowledge that no more of the world's resources have been depleted for it, no more of the environment has been damaged, and no more cruelty has taken place. Plus, you're saving it from going to the landfill.

Secondhand shops contain more exciting variety than new clothing shops, and perusing them

Putting together a cruelty-free look on a budget? Secondhand clothes stores are the places to go. Just be mindful of the microfiber issue.

really can be like a treasure hunt. What's more, the prices are usually great. There are a couple of things to think about when it comes to second-hand buying, though.

If you don't want to wear new clothes made from animal products—fur, leather, and silk, for example—how do you feel about wearing those clothes when they're secondhand? The animal has already died, but many people feel that by wearing clothes made from animal products, they're still promoting that product and that look.

If you have strong feelings about microfibers, be aware that secondhand synthetic clothes shed even more microfibers than new synthetic clothes. The older these clothes get, the more microfibers they release every time they're washed. If you do decide to buy secondhand synthetics, it's worth considering what you could do with those clothes that doesn't involve washing them too much.

LOOK AT THE LABELS

If you want to be sure you're buying clothes that have been made ethically, the best way is to look for labels that certify they've met certain standards—although it's worth remembering that certification can cost a lot of money, and there are small businesses out there that may be operating according to strong ethical values but just can't afford certification.

FAIR TRADE AND ORGANIC CERTIFICATION

There are two major fair trade certification labels to check for—the World Fair Trade Organization (WFTO) label and the Fairtrade Labeling Organizations International (FLO) label.

For organic clothes (especially cotton and wool), the Global Organic Textile Standard (GOTS) is the world's best-recognized label, and fabrics or garments that sport this label will have been made according to rigorous ethical, labor-related, and environmental standards.

If you see this certification label on a garment—the Global Organic Textile Standard (GOTS)—you can rest assured it's been produced to international standards of ethics.

OTHER ECOLABELS

There are many less well-known certification pro-
grams around the world that guarantee garments
have been made according to particular standards.

If you see a garment with a particular ecolabel and
would like to know more about what it means or if you
want to search for what ecolabels are out there, visit
http://www.ecolabelindex.com.

IF THE PRICE IS RIGHT

Ethical clothes can come at a premium. It is more
expensive to make clothes in ethical ways, and not
everyone can afford to buy fair trade and organic.
Buying fewer clothes helps, and then you'll have
more money to spend on each individual item.
Nonetheless, the prices will remain out of range for
some people.

If you have the money to spend on fair trade and
organic clothes, it's wonderful to use it. You're encour-
aging the growth of ethical clothing businesses and
thus helping the world. But it's also great to stay aware
that you're in a privileged position to be able to do so.

KNOW WHAT YOU'RE BUYING

Check all the labels pinned to a garment as well as
those inside it—they should say exactly what the fabric is, as well as give any certification information.

PERSONAL SCORECARD

Everyone has his or her own personal values that are most important to him or her. How can you sort through all this information and make wardrobe decisions that you are comfortable with? One way is by making a personal scorecard. You can take it shopping and refer to it to decide what you will and won't buy*.

I will buy ...	Never	Now & then	Anytime	Only secondhand	Only if it's guaranteed to be ...
Wool					
Alpaca					
Angora					
Mohair					
Cashmere					
Silk					
Cotton					
Linen					
Ramie					
Hemp					
Synthetics (Polyester, acrylic, spandex)					
Rayon					
Lyocell					
Bamboo					
Soy					
Fur, leather, sheepskin					

*If there are any companies that you feel have deeply unethical practices and that you want to avoid buying from, add them to your scorecard, too.

If you want to know more about where, how, and of what a garment was made, then make a point of asking the store owner. Even the act of asking is a powerful statement. You're letting the store owner know that their customers care about these things—and that can be influential.

BUY THE FIBER, MAKE THE FASHION

Do you sew, knit, weave, or crochet? It may be cost effective to buy ethically sourced fabric or yarn and make your own beautiful, cruelty-free clothes.

If you don't sew, don't despair! Sometimes all you need for a beautiful, ethical garment is the fabric itself. Buy a length of organic or fair trade cotton and then do an internet search for "no sew" skirts, dresses, and tops. There are some good-looking and versatile ideas out there.

If you struggle to find clothes in stores that meet your ethical standards, why not take matters into your own hands and sew your own?

Chapter Five

BEYOND BUYING

Your power as a conscious consumer of fashion doesn't end with the purchases you make. The way you care for your clothes and the way you talk to other people about clothes matters, too.

CARING FOR YOUR CLOTHES

You might be surprised how much of an impact you can make when you care for your clothes thoughtfully. First of all, make sure you know the recommended ways to wash and dry your particular garments. Sticking to these will help them last as long as possible. You should find washing instructions in any new garment you buy. This website will help you interpret what a number of the symbols mean: https://www .polti-usa.com/reading-clothing-labels.

There are also other reasons to think carefully about washing and drying. They use large amounts of energy, and household electricity use is one of the greatest contributors to greenhouse gases, which are driving climate change. Cambridge University's *Well Dressed*

Report investigated the energy use involved in a typical T-shirt's life cycle. They found that 60 percent of the total energy used over the T-shirt's life (including its manufacture, distribution, use, and disposal) comes from the "use" phase—meaning what you do with it after you buy it. The study took into account machine washing, tumble drying, and ironing and based their calculations on the T-shirt being washed twenty-five times at 140 degrees Fahrenheit (60 degrees Celsius).

The report recommends that to be more eco-friendly, we need to wash our clothes less often and at lower temperatures. We also need to hang dry them rather than tumble dry them, and avoid ironing if we possibly can.

The ethical-clothing journey doesn't end at the store checkout. You can help the world by also thinking about how you wash and dry your clothes.

MANAGING MICROFIBERS

To refresh, microfibers come from synthetic clothes and are poisoning our waterways, coastlines, and oceans. Manufacturers are working on coatings that stop synthetic fabrics from shedding their microfibers in the wash, and experiments with waterless washing machines also look promising. However, it could take some time for these innovations to hit

ECO LAUNDRY PRODUCTS

Many laundry products, including laundry soap, stain removers, and fabric softeners, contain an array of toxic chemicals. These can include fragrances, stabilizers, bleach, brighteners, phosphates, and more. Every time you wash your clothes, these chemicals are flowing out into the environment.

What can you do? Whenever possible, buy safe, eco-friendly laundry products. You can replace fabric softener with vinegar and brighteners with baking soda. And you'll find numerous ideas for making your own eco-friendly laundry soap on the internet.

Jessica Alba cofounded the Honest Company, a health-friendly personal care brand. The company's legal battles expose how tough it can be for ethical companies to compete in today's profit-focused world.

the mainstream market. So what can you do now? Some simple tips are:

- Wash any synthetic clothes as little as you can, for as short a time as you can, and on the coolest temperature you can. High temperatures are likely to loosen microfibers.
- Use liquid laundry soaps, rather than laundry powders (especially any that have with extra oxidizing agents for stain removal). Studies show these also loosen microfibers.
- Dispose of the lint from your dryer responsibly. If you're drying synthetics, it'll be full of microfibers, so don't wash this lint down the drain!

If you have some money to spend, it's worthwhile to buy a lint filter for your washing machine—and clear it regularly.

Recently, antimicrofiber washing bags have also arrived on the market. You simply put your synthetic clothes inside the bag for washing, take them out afterward, and then remove the accumulated lint from the seams of the bag (and dispose of it safely.) These are an excellent investment on behalf of all freshwater and sea life!

TALK TO THE MAKERS

One of the most powerful ways to push for change in the fashion industry is by going directly to the people who make or sell garments, asking them questions and telling them your concerns.

Is there a new small fashion business getting off the ground in your area? A new boutique or clothing label? When a business is just starting out, that is a great time to tell them the values you'd love to see them promote. Ask them all about how they will source their materials or garments, and let them know what issues are important to you. Let them know that you'll sing their praises to everyone you know if they prioritize ethical clothing.

Everything we do on land affects the ocean, and without a healthy ocean, life on land cannot survive. We need clean oceans, teeming with healthy animal and plant life.

Research clothing brands you love, and find out whether there are any problematic ethical practices involved in their supply chain. Then send them an email or a message on social media. (Social media can be especially effective because your question, and their reply, will be public.) Tell them all the things you like about them, and also tell them what you'd love to see them change.

When a company makes a change for the better, send them messages of appreciation. This kind of positive reinforcement helps them feel good about their decision and stick to it—and encourages other companies to follow suit.

THE FUTURE OF FASHION

What does the fashion world look like in your ideal future? Which fibers are most popular? What new technologies have been developed? What does a successful fashion business look like? Who makes the clothes and how? Which clothes fill your own wardrobe?

The exciting thing is that by making conscious choices for your own wardrobe and spreading your ideas among your friends and the wider community, you really can help make this future happen.

With the internet, you have the power to research clothing companies. Why not try contacting them? You might influence them in positive ways.

10 GREAT QUESTIONS TO ASK A MAKER/SELLER

1. What is this garment made of?

2. If it's made from wool or another animal fiber, how were those animals treated on the farm?

3. If it's a plant or animal fiber, is it organic?

4. Is it fair trade?

5. Does it come with any other certification or guarantees?

6. Where was this dyed and using what method? What is the dye process and the specific factory's impact on its local environment?

7. What country was this sewn in, and who made it? How are the workers treated in the factory or business where this was made?

8. How well made is this garment, and how long will it last?

9. What are the businesses involved in making this garment doing to make their practices more ethical and to lessen the harm they do to the planet?

10. What are you doing to make your own practices more ethical? Would you consider making or selling 100 percent cruelty-free clothing?

GLOSSARY

abattoir Where animals are sent to be slaughtered.

artisan Relating to skilled handcrafts.

aspirational Something to aim toward.

biodegrade To rot or break down naturally.

by-product A product that is made in the process of making another one.

carcinogenic Cancer causing.

castration The removal of the testes, rendering a male incapable of reproducing.

cellulose An insoluble material that the cell walls of plants are made of.

denim A type of cotton that is twill woven, tough, and most commonly dyed blue.

domesticated Trained or bred to be useful to or dependent upon humans.

fiber Threads from which textiles can be made.

fleece The wool or hair that covers an animal such as a sheep, goat, or alpaca.

flock A group of animals, often sheep or goats.

landfill Where garbage and waste is commonly dumped.

larvae The juvenile form of an insect before it undergoes its metamorphosis.

overconsumption Using too many of the world's resources to be sustainable.

pesticides Substances used to kill pests, usually insects or other invertebrates.

residues Leftover traces of a substance.

shearer A person who clips or removes fleece from an animal.

sustainable Able to be continued without causing damage or degradation.

synthetic Artificial or human made.

textiles Cloth or fabric.

FOR MORE INFORMATION

EcoCult
Website: https://ecocult.com
Facebook: @ecocultnyc
Twitter and Instagram: @ecocult
EcoCult is a guide to sustainable fashion and lifestyle
in New York City.

Ethical Fashion Forum
3 Princes Street, 1st Floor
London W1B 2LD
United Kingdom
+44 (0)20 7018 3738
Website: http://www.ethicalfashionforum.com
This industry body for sustainable fashion is a great
place to find out who's doing what in the field.

Fair Trade USA
1500 Broadway, Suite 400
Oakland, CA 94612
(510) 663-5260
Website: https://www.fairtradecertified.org
Facebook: @fairtradecertified
Twitter: @fairtradecert
Instagram: @fairtradeusa
This nonprofit organization sets standards and cer-
tifies fair trade products. The website contains

shopping guides and ideas for supporting fair trade in your community.

Fashion Heroes
Website: http://fashionheroes.eco
Fashion Heroes supports, promotes, and celebrates those who are working toward ecofashion. Their website is packed with information about ethical brands and upcoming events.

Fashion Revolution
19 Dig Street
Ashbourne, Derbyshire DE6 1GF
United Kingdom
Website: http://fashionrevolution.org
Facebook: @fashionrevolution.org
Twitter: @Fash_Rev
Instagram: @fash_rev
This activist movement organizes events and campaigns around the world to push for a kinder, more sustainable, and ethical fashion industry.

Fashion Takes Action
Website: https://fashiontakesaction.com
Facebook and Instagram: @fashiontakesaction
Twitter: @FTAorg
Fashion Takes Action is a Canadian organization leading a range of initiatives to increase the fashion industry's sustainability.

Project JUST
40 Worth Street, Suite 303
New York, NY 10013
Website: https://projectjust.com
Facebook and Instagram: @projectjust
Twitter: @project_just
This organization researches the practices of fashion
   companies extensively, makes their findings avail-
   able to shoppers, and awards its seal of approval
   only to companies that meet the highest standards.

Trusted Clothes
Old Boehmer Box Factory
283 Duke Street W, #214
Kitchener, ON N2H 3X7
Canada
+1 226 476 1438
Website: https://www.trustedclothes.com
Facebook: @TrustedClothes
Twitter and Instagram: @trustedclothes
This Canadian organization advocates for a more
   "ethical, sustainable and health-conscious" cloth-
   ing and fashion industry. They look for enthusiastic
   volunteers from anywhere in the world.

FOR FURTHER READING

Bartley, Tim, Sebastian Koos, Hiram Samuel, Gustavo Setrini, and Nik Summers. *Looking Behind the Label: Global Industries and the Conscientious Consumer (Global Research Studies)*. Bloomington, IN: Indiana University Press, 2015.

David, Alison Matthews. *Fashion Victims: The Dangers of Dress Past and Present.* London, UK: Bloomsbury Academic, 2015.

Fashionary. *Fashionpedia—The Visual Dictionary of Fashion Design.* Kwun Tong, Hong Kong: Fashionary, 2016.

Fine, Doug. *Hemp Bound: Dispatches from the Front Lines of the Next Agricultural Revolution.* Hartford, VT: Chelsea Green Publishing, 2014.

Köhrer, Ellen, and Magdalena Schaffrin. *Fashion Made Fair: Modern#Innovative#Sustainable.* Munich, Germany: Prestel, 2016.

Ricard, Matthieu. *A Plea for the Animals: The Moral, Philosophical, and Evolutionary Imperative to Treat All Beings with Compassion.* Boulder, CO: Shambhala, 2016.

Wild, Denise. *Mend & Make Fabulous.* Fort Collins, CO: Interweave, 2014.

Wilson, Rosie. *Fashion Industry* (A Closer Look: Global Industries). New York, NY: Rosen Publishing, 2010.

Yamase, Koko. *Cut-Up Couture: Edgy Upcycled Garments to Sew.* Fort Collins, CO: Interweave, 2012.

BIBLIOGRAPHY

Fair Trade International. Retrieved November 17, 2017. https://www.fairtrade.net.

Global Organic Textile Standard. Retrieved November 17, 2017. http://www.global-standard.org.

International Wool Textile Organization. Retrieved November 17, 2017. http://www.iwto.org.

Kaye, Leon. "Clothing to Dye For: The Textile Sector Must Confront Water Risks." *The Guardian*. Retrieved November 17, 2017. https://www.theguardian.com/sustainable-business/dyeing-textile-sector-water-risks-adidas.

McIlvride, David, and Roger Williams. *RiverBlue*. 2016. http://riverbluethemovie.eco.

McQuaile, Jenny. *Straight Curve*. 2017. http://www.straightcurvefilm.com.

Morgan, Andrew. *The True Cost*. 2015. https://truecostmovie.com.

O'Sullivan, Niall J., Matthew D. Teasdale, Valeria Mattiangeli, Frank Maixner, Ron Pinhasi, Daniel G. Bradley, and Albert Zink. "A Whole Mitochondria Analysis of the Tyrolean Iceman's Leather Provides Insights into the Animal Sources of Copper Age Clothing." Nature.com, August 2016. https://www.nature.com/articles/srep31279.

PETA's Shopping Guide to Compassionate Clothing. Retrieved November 17, 2017. https://www.peta.org/living/fashion/cruelty-free-clothing-guide.

The Story of Stuff Project. *The Story of Microfibers*. Retrieved November 17, 2017. http://storyofstuff .org/movies/story-of-microfibers.

Toups, Melissa A., Andrew Kitchen, Jessica E. Light, David L. Reed. "Origin of Clothing Lice Indicated Early Clothing Use by Anatomically Modern Humans in Africa." *Molecular Biology and Evolution*, January 2011.

Trampe, Debra, Diederik A. Stapel, and Frans W. Siero. "The Self-Activation Effect of Advertisements: Ads Can Affect Whether and How Consumers Think About the Self." *Journal of Consumer Research*. Retrieved November 17, 2017. http:// www.acrwebsite.org/volumes/v36/NAACR _vol36_29.pdf.

University of Cambridge Institute for Manufacturing. *Well-Dressed*? Cambridge, UK: University of Cambridge. https://www.ifm.eng.cam.ac.uk/uploads /Resources/Other_Reports/UK_textiles.pdf.

Watts, Andrew J. R., Mauricio A. Urbina, Shauna Corr, Ceri Lewis, and Tamara S. Galloway. "Ingestion of Plastic Microfibers by the Crab *Carcinus maenas* and Its Effect on Food Consumption and Energy Balance." *Environmental Science & Technology*, December 2015.

World Fairtrade Organization. Retrieved November 17, 2017. https://www.wfto.com.

World Wildlife Fund—Cotton Industries. Retrieved November 17, 2017. https://www.worldwildlife.org /industries/cotton.

INDEX

ABOUT THE AUTHOR

Johanna Knox is a New Zealand author and journalist who has been writing about sustainable living for ten years. She is addicted to secondhand clothes, and her daughter has picked up the bug as well. Together they make a formidable thrift-shopping duo. They live with a fluffy gray cat called Smoofy, whose molted fur Knox would like to try spinning one day.

PHOTO CREDITS

Cover Richard Levine/Corbis News/Getty Images; p. 5 Glow Decor/Glow/Getty Images; p. 8 Callista Images/Culture/Getty Images; p. 9 Tobias Bernhard/Oxford Scientific/Getty Images; p. 14 James L. Amos/NATIONAL GEOGRAPHIC IMAGE COLLECTION/Getty Images; p. 17 James R.T. Bossert/Shutterstock.com; p. 21 Tony Hertz/Passage/Getty Images; p. 23 Lawrence K. Ho/Los Angeles Times/Getty Images; p. 25 DEA/E. Giovenzana/De Agostini/Getty Images; p. 28 Matt Anderson Photography/Moment/Getty Images; p. 31 Nathan Benn/Corbis Historical/Getty Images; p. 33 Bloomberg/Getty Images; p. 36 Luciano Mortuia/Shutterstock.com; p. 39 Melodie Jeng/Getty Images; p. 41 Marbury/Shutterstock.com; p. 43 Thomas Trutschel/Photothek/Getty Images; p. 46 Andy Crawford, Steve Garden/Dorling Kindersley/Getty Images; p. 48 Monkey Business Images/Shutterstock.com; p. 49 Stefanie Keenan/WireImage/Getty Images; p. 51 Dmitry Polonskly/Shutterstock.com; p. 52 GaudiLab/Shutterstock.com; back cover, interior pages background pattern (leaf) mexrix/Shutterstock.com; interior pages background pattern (bamboo) wow.subtropica/Shutterstock.com

Design and Layout: Tahara Anderson; Editor: Carolyn DeCarlo; Photo Researcher: Nicole Baker